Arctic Peoples

Mir Tamim Ansary

Heinemann Library
Des Plaines, Illinois

© 2000 Reed Educational & Professional Publishing
Published by Heinemann Library,
an imprint of Reed Educational & Professional Publishing,
1350 East Touhy Avenue, Suite 240 West
Des Plaines, IL 60018

Customer Service: 888-454-2279

Designed by Depke Design

Printed in Hong Kong

04 03 02 01 00
10 9 8 7 6 5 4 3 2 1

Library of Congress Cataloging-in-Publication Data
Ansary, Mir Tamim.
　　Arctic peoples / Mir Tamim Ansary.
　　　　p. cm. – (Native Americans)
　　Includes bibliographical references and index.
　　Summary: Describes various elements of the traditional life of
Arctic people including their homes, clothing, games, crafts, and
beliefs as well as changes brought about by the arrival of
Europeans.
　　ISBN 1-57572-920-2 (lib. bdg.)
　　1. Eskimos Juvenile literature. 2. Inuit Juvenile literature.
3. Aleuts Juvenile literature. [1. Eskimos. 2. Inuit.
3. Aleuts.] I. Title. II. Series: Ansary, Mir Tamim. Native
Americans.
E99.E7A68 1999
979.8'004971—dc21   99-17407
　　　　　　　　　　　　　　　　　　　　　　　　　　　　　CIP

Acknowledgments
The publisher would like to thank the following for permission to reproduce photographs:
Cover: Chris Arend
Dr. E.R. Degginger, p. 4; The Granger Collection, pp. 7, 21, 24, 25; Stock Montage, Inc., p. 8; Animals Animals/Johnny
Johnson, p. 9; Eugene Fisher, pp. 10, 11, 19, 27, 28; Corbis-Bettmann, pp. 12, 23; UPI/Corbis-Bettmann, pp. 13, 14;
Hudson's Bay Company Archives/Provincial Archives of Manitoba, pp. 15, 16; Robert Peary, p. 18; Earth Scenes/Shane
Moore, p. 20; American Museum of Natural History/A. Anik & J. Beckett, p. 22; National Geographic Society/Chris
Johns, p. 26; Indian and Northern Affairs Canada, p. 29; CP Picture Archive/Bill Becker, p. 30 top; John Reeves, p. 30
bottom

Our special thanks to Lana Grant, Native American MLS, for her help
in the preparation of this book.

Note to the Reader Some words are shown in bold, **like this.** You can find
out what they mean by looking in the glossary.

Contents

Land of Ice and Snow

The circle of land around the North Pole is called the Arctic. Here in the far north, summers are short. Winters are long and very cold. In December, the sun hardly comes up at all. The sea is covered with ice, and even the ground is frozen hard.

During the short summer, the ice melts. The ground turns to mud. A few plants **sprout** up, but not enough for people to eat. You may think that no one could live here—but you'd be wrong. People have lived in the Arctic for thousands of years.

North Pole

Arctic Circle

Arctic peoples

North America

Equator

From Asia to America

The people of the American Arctic came from Asia perhaps 8,000 years ago. The Aleuts, also called the Unangan, came by boat. They paddled along the Aleutian Islands. This chain of islands stretches between Alaska and Asia. The Aleuts settled on these islands and on the nearby Alaskan coast.

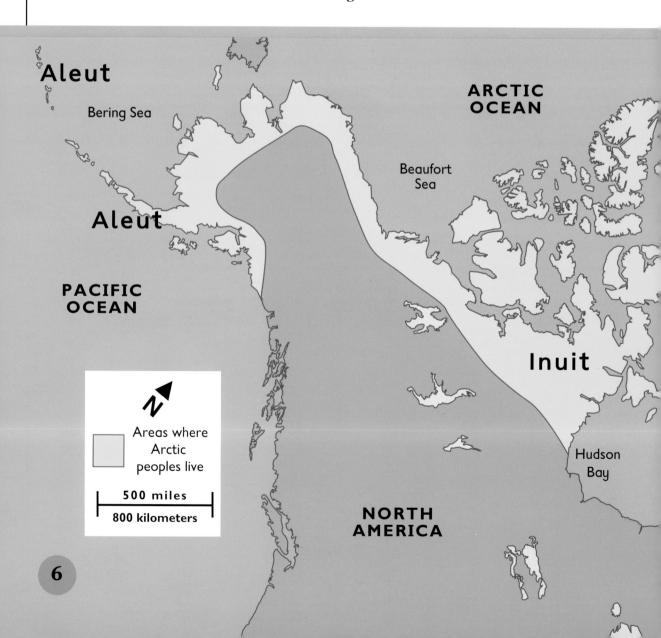

Aleut

Bering Sea

ARCTIC OCEAN

Beaufort Sea

Aleut

Inuit

PACIFIC OCEAN

Areas where Arctic peoples live

500 miles
800 kilometers

Hudson Bay

NORTH AMERICA

Other people walked to America around that same time. They walked on the ice that covered the sea. These people call themselves the Inuit. Some people call them Eskimos. The Inuit kept spreading east. They now live in the American Arctic, from Alaska to Greenland.

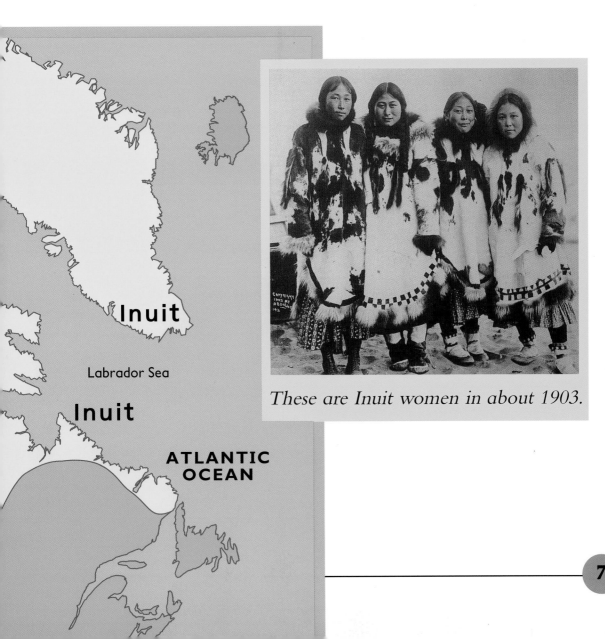

Inuit

Labrador Sea

Inuit

ATLANTIC OCEAN

These are Inuit women in about 1903.

Hunters on Land and Sea

The Inuit and Aleuts ate no grains, vegetables, or plants of any kind. They got all their food from animals. They speared fish. They hunted whales, walruses, and seals. When they killed an animal, they used every part of it for something.

This Inuit hunter is sneaking up on a seal.

Musk oxen have thick fur that helps them live in the cold Arctic.

Some Inuit traveled inland, away from the coast. There, they hunted big land animals. They killed **caribou,** musk oxen, and even polar bears. They made their weapons out of the animals they hunted. They used bones, horns, **tusks,** and teeth. From these parts, they made spears, arrows, and **harpoons.**

Kayaks and Dog Sleds

The Arctic people go to sea in one-person boats called kayaks. A kayak is made of animal skins stretched over a wooden frame. The kayaker sits in a small opening. The boater's coat fits over the opening like a lid. If the kayak tips over, it still floats. The boater can tip it back up.

The kayaker's coat fits snugly over the hole to keep out water.

A well-trained team of huskies can pull a sled 20 miles (32 kilometers) per hour.

On long hunts across the snow, the Inuit traveled by dog sled. They made the sled runners out of **ivory**. Strong dogs called huskies pulled the sleds. Huskies have such thick fur, they can swim without getting wet. They can sleep in snow without getting cold.

Arctic Homes

The Arctic people even built houses out of animal parts. They stretched animal skins over frames made of bones. For windows, they used seal gut. Seal gut is like clear plastic when it is stretched—light shines through it. The Inuit also built houses out of rocks or **sod.**

This tentlike house is made of sealskin.

These Inuit are using hard, well-packed snow to make an igloo.

On long winter hunts, some Inuit built igloos to live in. An igloo is a dome-shaped house made out of blocks of snow. A fire in the middle makes it warm. People sit and sleep on piles of cozy fur. Sometimes two or more igloos were connected by tunnels.

Cold Weather Clothing

The Inuit invented a hooded coat known as a parka. They wore knee-high boot covers called mukluks. Their clothes were loose except at the wrists, neck, and ankles. Their body heat warmed up the air inside these clothes. Mothers carried their babies inside their shirts.

Sealskin outfits keep this Inuit couple warm.

Sunlight on snow can be very bright. So the Inuit made snow goggles with slits for seeing through. They made shoes with **cleats** of bone. Cleats helped them climb on ice without slipping. They invented snow shoes, which look like tennis rackets. These helped the Inuit walk on snow without sinking.

These snow goggles are made of wood.

Group Life

The Aleuts lived in villages. They were divided into **ranks,** with a chief at the top. But the Inuit had a very different way of life. They lived in groups of about 30 people. Each group was one big family. Inuit groups moved from place to place during the year.

The Inuit had no chiefs, no government, and no tribes. Each group was on its own. Some people in a group were seen as leaders because they were wise. But these leaders could not give orders. They could only give advice. No one had to obey them.

Inuit families spent much of their time traveling from place to place.

Games and Crafts

Life in the Arctic was hard but not gloomy. The Inuit invented many sports to play in their small huts. The head pull, for example, is still played. In this game, two people lie on the ground. They grab each other's heads to try to pull each other across a line.

Wrestling is also a popular sport among the Inuit today.

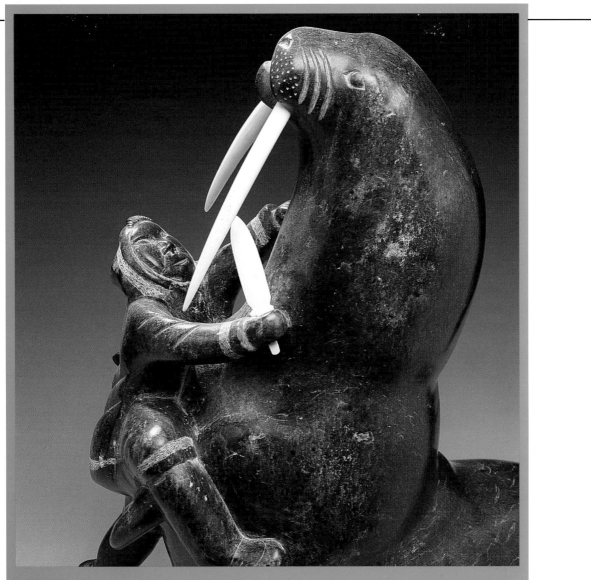

This sculpture is carved from ivory and a soft, white stone called soapstone.

The Inuit filled their hard life with beauty, too. Inuit artists carve figures out of **ivory** and soapstone. They make jewelry out of shells and feathers. They make masks, which are used to act out stories. Many Inuit stories tell tales about **spirits,** beings who cannot be seen.

Acting Out Stories

Inuit beliefs say the world is full of **spirits.** There is Sedna, for example. According to Inuit stories, her parents were giants. As a baby, she tried to eat her parents. They threw her into the sea. Her fingers became the millions of fish. Then she grew into a giant and is living down there still.

Colored lights, called the aurora borealis, sometimes fill the Arctic sky, giving viewers a sense of mystery and beauty.

Other ancient stories tell about the "people of the sky." In these Inuit tales, the sun is a lovely girl. She carries a **torch.** The moon is her brother, a great hunter. He keeps chasing his sister across the sky because he wants that torch.

This Inuit mask stands for a sky spirit.

21

The Spirit World

According to Inuit beliefs, people live on as spirits after they die. So the Inuit believe their ancestors live among them as spirits. These spirits can bring bad luck if they are cold and hungry. In early times, the Inuit often set a little food aside for their ancestors, even when they had very little.

An Inuit artist joined several pieces of carved bone to make this death mask.

An angakok may wear a special costume to get in touch with spirits.

The angakok is an Inuit religious person. The Inuit believe he or she can get in touch with spirits. These spirits can heal sick people or bring good luck. When help is needed, a family gathers in a circle. The angakok sings and plays a drum to bring a spirit near.

Europeans Arrive

In 1576, an English sailor named Martin Frobisher landed in the Arctic. He told people in England that he had found gold there. Europeans started flocking to the land of the Inuit. They found no gold, but they did find seals and whales. Seal fur and whale oil were worth money.

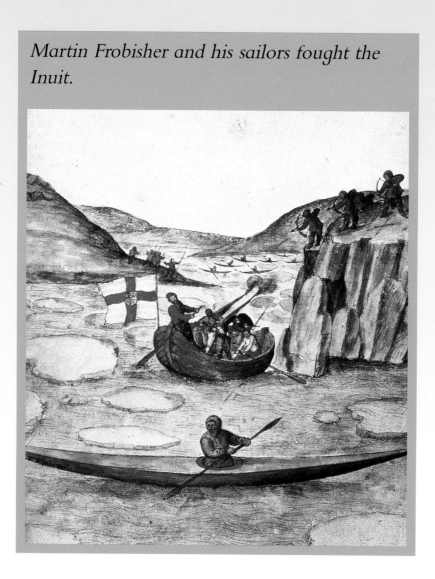

Martin Frobisher and his sailors fought the Inuit.

The Europeans and their decendants killed whales in great numbers.

The Inuit started trading with the Europeans. They traded fur and oil for European goods. And European hunters killed many animals, too. The Arctic way of life began to change. In the west, Russian fur traders made the Aleuts into their slaves. The Aleuts suffered many hardships under Russian rule.

A Changing Culture

Missionaries followed the traders and hunters. By 1900, the Aleuts had all joined the Greek Orthodox Church. On the **mainland,** missionaries built schools. They tried to make the Aletus and Inuit speak only English. They tried to make them forget their old ways. They succeeded for a time.

This church near Anchorage, Alaska, was built around 1845.

This Inuit man prepares for a winter journey on an ATV—an all-terrain vehicle.

The Inuit and Aleuts no longer live in tents or igloos. Most live in wooden houses. Many still hunt for a living, but they now use modern tools. They have rifles instead of bows or **harpoons.** They travel by snowmobile instead of dog sled.

The American Arctic Today

Today, however, the Arctic people are working to keep their old ways alive. The Inuit language is taught in many Arctic schools. The Inuit have a computer center at Rankin Inlet, a town on Hudson Bay. Arctic children can read Inuit stories on the Internet. They can learn about Inuit customs by computer.

Inuit children at Rankin Inlet often use the Internet to learn.

28

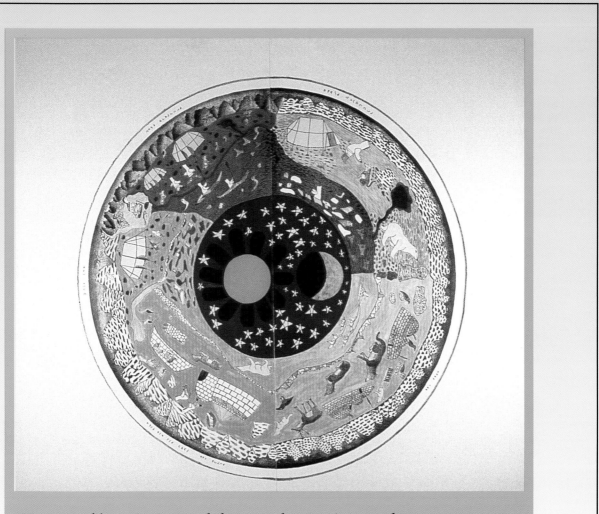

Kenojuak's painting celebrates the Inuit people.

In Canada a new territory has been set up which
rules itself. It is called Nunavut (noo-na-voot).
Most of the people in Nunavut are Inuit. This
painting was done by the Inuit artist Kenojuak.
It celebrates the new Inuit territory. It celebrates
Inuit hopes for the future.

Famous Arctic People

Susan Aglukark (Inuit: 1967–) Musical star Aglukark sings in both English and Inuktitut. Her albums *Arctic Rose* and *This Child* were big hits in Canada. Her video "Searching" won a Much Music award. In 1993, *Maclean's Magazine* named Aglukark one of "Canada's 100 Leaders To Watch."

Jack Anawak (Inuit: 1950–) Anawak became famous as a hunter and businessman. Then he went into politics. In 1988, he was elected to Canada's House of Commons, the group that makes the nation's laws. The area Anawak represented is now part of Nunavut.

Kenojuak Ashevak (1927–) This famous artist grew up in the Arctic. In the late 1950's, she began drawing and carving in soapstone. Since then, her work has been shown around the world. A movie was made about her life in 1961. Her picture *The Enchanted Owl* appears on a Canadian stamp.

Glossary

caribou type of large reindeer

cleats nail-like bumps on the bottom of a shoe

harpoon spearlike weapon with big hooks at the end

inland part of a country that is not near the coast

ivory hard white bonelike material that most tusks are made of

mainland largest part of a continent

missionaries people who try to get others to join their religion

rank higher or lower position in a group

sod soil held together by grass roots

spirits beings that have life but cannot be seen

sprout to begin to grow

territory part of a nation that rules itself

torch flaming stick

tribe large group of families who share the same leaders, religious beliefs, and traditions

tusk long tooth that sticks out of the mouth of many elephants and walruses

More Books to Read

Reynolds, Jan. *Frozen Land.* San Diego, Cal: Harcourt Brace & Company, 1993.

Siska, Heather S. *People of the Ice: How the Inuit Lived.* Buffalo, NY: Firefly Books, 1992.

Thomson, Ruth. *The Inuit.* Danbury, Conn: Children's Press, 1996.

Index